LEONARD BERNSTEIN

A Passion for Music

LEONARD BERNSTEIN

A Passion for Music

JOHANNA HURWITZ

Illustrated by Sonia O. Lisker

THE JEWISH PUBLICATION SOCIETY

Philadelphia and Jerusalem   5754/1993

The publication of this volume has been made possible by a grant from the Billy Rose Foundation.

Library of Congress Cataloging-in-Publication Data
Hurwitz, Johanna.
Leonard Bernstein : a passion for music / Johanna Hurwitz ;
illustrated by Sonia O. Lisker.
p.   cm.
Includes bibliographical references and index.
Summary: Traces the life and career of the famous composer,
conductor, pianist, and teacher.
ISBN 0–8276–0501–3
1. Bernstein, Leonard, 1918–90—Juvenile literature.   2. Musicians—
United States—Biography—Juvenile literature.   [1. Bernstein,
Leonard, 1918–90.   2. Musicians.]   I. Lisker, Sonia O., ill.
II. Title.
ML3930.B48H87   1993
780'.92—dc20
[B]   93–2592
                                              CIP
                                              AC MN

10   9   8   7   6   5   4   3   2   1

CONTENTS

1   *A Musical Child*   3

2   *An American Education*   14

3   *Conductor Lenny Bernstein*   24

4   *An American Composer*   40

5   *An American Phenomenon*   50

IMPORTANT DATES   61

AUTHOR'S NOTE   65

BIBLIOGRAPHY   67

INDEX   69

LEONARD
BERNSTEIN

A Passion for Music

1

A Musical Child

Every day in homes around this country, there are parents who question and scold their children. "Have you practiced your music lesson yet? You can't watch any television until you do your practicing. Go and practice. Now!"

When Leonard Bernstein was growing up, his father scolded him, too. But the message was very different. Leonard's father, Sam Bernstein, yelled at him to *stop* practicing the piano. Sam, the son of a rabbi, was an immigrant from Russia. He had come alone to the United States in 1908 when he was sixteen years old. He spent his first two years in this country supporting himself by cleaning fish twelve hours a day, six days a week. Later, he worked in a barbershop owned by an uncle. From there he got a job selling supplies to other barbershops and beauty parlors. The only musicians Sam Bernstein

*Sam didn't want him to become a poor musician
playing to earn his supper.*

ever knew were the *klezmers*. These were strolling performers in eastern Europe who searched for weddings and bar mitzvah celebrations where they could play their music. In return, the *klezmers* were paid small sums of money and given free meals. To Sam Bernstein, these musicians were hardly better than beggars. So when young Leonard spent long hours practicing the piano, it was no wonder that his father complained and told him to stop. Sam had big plans for his clever son. He wanted him to join him in his business. He certainly didn't want him to become a poor musician playing to earn his supper.

Leonard Bernstein was born near Boston, in Lawrence, Massachusetts, on August 25, 1918. He was the first of three children born to Sam and Jennie Bernstein. Although he was named Louis after his maternal grandfather, his parents preferred the name Leonard. That, or Lenny for short, is what they always called him.

When the time came for Lenny to begin school, he had a big surprise. His kindergarten teacher called "Louis Bernstein." Little Lenny looked around the room for the other boy in his class who had the same last name. He was amazed to discover that *he* was Louis. Despite the official school records, Lenny continued to use the name he and his parents liked better. It was not until he was sixteen years old and applying for his first driver's license, however, that he legally changed his name to Leonard.

Little Lenny was a thin and sickly child. He was allergic to cats and dust. Frequently he had bouts of bronchitis or, even worse, bad attacks of asthma. Then he would turn blue from lack of oxygen, and his parents worried that he was about to die. In addition to being frail, young Lenny was shy. The family moved often during his youth, and as a result, he didn't have any friends for several years. In time, however, he had a sister Shirley, who, although five years his junior, shared his interests. Their little brother Burton was thirteen years younger than Lenny. Throughout his life, Leonard always remained very close to both his siblings.

Even at an early age, Lenny showed a deep interest in music. As a toddler, when he heard music, Lenny would stop his crawling and react to the music by crying. Perhaps this was caused by a frustration that he could not be closer to the music and its source. At the age of four or five, Lenny stood at the windowsill and moved his fingers along the wooden ledge as if playing on an imaginary piano keyboard.

Whenever the family visited with friends or relatives who owned a piano, the instrument drew Lenny like a magnet pulling at a piece of iron. He pressed the keys and attempted to play little tunes for himself.

Lenny's father came from a religious background. Sam Bernstein's father and grandfather had been talmudic scholars, and Sam himself devoted much of his free time to reading the Talmud. When Lenny was nine years old, however, his father left the Orthodox synagogue to which he belonged and joined Mishkan Tefila, a Conservative congregation. It was at this temple that Lenny would in time become a bar mitzvah. Mishkan Tefila had an organ and a choir, which were not to be found at a traditional Orthodox shul. When he accom-

At four or five, he moved his fingers along the windowsill as if playing an imaginary piano.

panied his father to services at this new synagogue, Lenny found himself moved to tears by the music. It was Lenny's first exposure to live music as opposed to music heard on the radio or on a phonograph. As always, music seemed to touch Lenny and pull at him with a strong and unexpected force. For a time, Lenny was so impressed by both the cantor and the rabbi at this new synagogue that he considered becoming a rabbi himself when he grew up.

Neither Jennie nor Sam was especially musical. The Bernstein family did not own an instrument of any kind, although they did have a phonograph and records of popular music. So it was not until he was ten years old that Lenny had a chance to really make music himself. One day he returned home from his afterschool

Hebrew studies to make a fantastic discovery. An old upright piano was standing in the hallway of his family's apartment. It had not been there when Lenny had left for school that morning. Lenny's aunt, Sam's sister Clara, was getting divorced and moving from the Boston area to New York. The piano had been hers, but she didn't play it. So she had decided to pass this big and bulky piece of furniture on to her brother and his family. It was a momentous and exciting gift.

At once, Lenny was able to pick out the popular melodies he knew on the instrument. He loved the piano, and he told his parents that he wanted to take lessons.

Years later, Leonard Bernstein, remembering the gift of the piano and his first chance to make music, recalled, "Suddenly I found my world."

Soon it was arranged that Lenny would study with a neighbor's daughter, Frieda Karp. The lessons cost one dollar an hour. It was an amount that the Bernsteins could afford without a problem. Lenny loved playing the piano whenever possible. Before long, Sam began to complain. He worried that all this piano playing was keeping his son from his schoolwork. He would shout at him to stop playing. One night, the family was awakened at two o'clock in the morning by the sound of Lenny at the piano. When his father shouted and asked him what he was doing at such an absurd hour of the night, Lenny replied, "I have to do this. The sounds are in my head, and I have to get them out." With such a passion for music, it didn't take long until Lenny played the piano better than his teacher.

This should not have surprised his parents. From a

young age, it was obvious that their son was exceptionally bright and creative. He received excellent grades at school, and he was always full of original ideas.

Just about the same time that the family acquired the piano, Lenny had been reading about ancient Rome. It inspired him and his best friend, Eddie Ryack, to invent their own country. They called it Rybernia, a name they created by combining parts of their last names. They were the country's leaders and they proceeded to devise their own special national anthem and even a Rybernian language. This was understood only by the "citizens" of Rybernia. Other friends were able to apply for citizenship and learn the language. In time, Lenny's younger sister and brother, Shirley and Burton, joined in the game, which they continued for the rest of their lives.

At twelve, Leonard enrolled at the New England Conservatory of Music. Now his weekly lesson cost three dollars. This was also the time when he was entering seventh grade. After passing the competitive entrance examination, he was admitted to the Boston Latin School. There was no tuition charged at this special, well-known junior-senior high school for boys, established in 1635. The school had extremely high academic standards. All students studied Latin in addition to their other subjects, and they were given three hours of homework every night. There were weekly exams in all subjects, too. More than half of the boys were expected to flunk out of the school.

Lenny did almost no homework; but instead of failing, he was such a bright student that he remained at the top of his class. He did, however, spend much of his free time practicing the piano, for he was obsessed with music. He taught his sister Shirley how to play the instrument. He borrowed scores from the public library and became familiar with all sorts of music: popular, jazz, and classical.

It wasn't long before Lenny's growing involvement with music became a source of tension at home. His mother, Jennie, was proud of his talent, and the more her husband complained, the more she encouraged their son.

Lenny began giving piano lessons to other young people besides his sister. With the money he made teaching, he was able to pay the three-dollar fee for his piano lessons. For although Sam could afford the amount, he did not want to pay this higher price for.

He gave piano lessons to help pay for his own.

something he did not value. And Sam Bernstein certainly did not want to encourage his son's growing passion in this business of music.

Before long, Lenny was also able to find some jobs in pickup dance bands. Together with a saxophonist and a drummer, he formed a group that performed at weddings and bar mitzvahs. It seemed as if his father's fear was coming true. Here was Sam Bernstein's son on the road to becoming a *klezmer* musician.

Although Sam objected to Lenny's involvement with music, Sam purchased a grand piano for his son when Lenny was thirteen. It was a much better piano than the old upright from his aunt. Sam also took Lenny to hear his first real concerts at Symphony Hall in Boston. Together they attended a performance of the Boston Pops playing Ravel's *Bolero*. The tickets had been sold as a fund-raiser for the synagogue, so of course Sam had bought them. Another time, Sam took Lenny to hear a recital by Sergei Rachmaninoff, the famous pianist and composer. Sam was amazed to see how many people had paid to hear just one person playing the piano!

In time, Lenny once again needed the challenge of a new piano teacher. This time he went to audition with Heinrich Gebhard, who was considered to be the finest music teacher in the Boston area. Gebhard charged twenty-five dollars for a one-hour lesson. He listened to Lenny and felt that he was not yet ready to work with him. Instead, Lenny began to study with Gebhard's assistant, Helen Coates. Her fee was six dollars a lesson. She was so impressed, however, with the talent of her new student that she deliberately began to schedule his lesson at the end of her day. Then she permitted the hour session to stretch to two or even three hours, but her fee remained the same. It was the beginning of a long, long association between the two of them.

His music ability made Lenny the center of any party he attended. It was a new and wonderful sensation for the once-shy boy. For the rest of his life, Lenny retained the magnetism and charm that drew people to him. He amused his friends by playing jazz music on the piano or leading them in singing popular songs. "When I went to a party, I just ran for the piano as soon as I got in the door," Leonard Bernstein once commented. "And [I] stayed there until they threw me out. It was as if I didn't exist without music."

During summer vacations, he entertained his parents and their friends by staging elaborate musical productions. The summer he was fourteen, Lenny decided to put on a performance of *Carmen*. In Lenny's shortened version of the opera, the male roles were sung by girls and the female roles sung by Lenny and the other boys in the show, dressed as women. Lenny himself was Carmen, and he wore a wig that had been donated by Sam Bernstein from his hair supply company.

Two summers later, Lenny organized a production of the Gilbert and Sullivan operetta *The Mikado*. This time the girls sang the female parts and Lenny's sister Shirley had the female lead of Yum-Yum. Lenny had the male lead of Nanki-Poo. The success of *The Mikado* encouraged Lenny to do *H.M.S. Pinafore*, another Gilbert and Sullivan operetta, the following summer.

The businessman in Sam could not help but admire his son's organizational abilities and initiative. He continued to hope that in time Lenny would outgrow his passion for music and eventually join his business of selling hair supplies. Lenny had changed from a frail, shy boy to a handsome young man with loads of energy and a lively personality. Someday, thought Sam, he would make a wonderful salesman if he put his mind to it.

2

An American Education

Sam Bernstein's business was doing well. Yet even if his son were to join him selling hair products, Sam Bernstein, like most Jewish parents, valued a good education. So he and Jennie were pleased when their son was accepted as an undergraduate at Harvard. He entered the freshman class in the fall of 1935. Although his father hoped he would study economics, Lenny persuaded Sam to let him major in music. In addition to his music courses, Lenny took many courses in literature and philosophy.

At Harvard, Lenny met many outstanding musicians. Some were young and just entering the music world. But there he met two established musicians who were especially influential in Lenny's future career. The first was the American composer Aaron Copland, who was to become his good friend. Copland was impressed with Lenny's obvious talent and suggested that he think about becoming a composer. At the same time, Lenny also met the conductor Dimitri Mitropoulos, who called Lenny a "genius boy" and told him that he should become a conductor.

Still another good friend that Lenny made during his college years was Adolph Green. The two young men met when Lenny was the music counselor at a summer camp in Pittsfield, Massachusetts. Lenny's big project for the campers was a production of the Gilbert and Sullivan operetta *The Pirates of Penzance*. Adolph Green, who lived in the Bronx in New York, was brought in to play a major role in the show. Although Adolph had no formal musical training, he impressed Lenny with his exceptional musical memory. Adolph was able to sing all the musical parts played by each instrument from every symphonic work he had ever heard.

When Lenny graduated from college in 1939, he was not eager to begin working for his father. Sam hoped that when his son saw how difficult it was to earn a living as a musician, he would reconcile himself to work in the Sam Bernstein Hair Company. In the past, a young American interested in a career in music would have immediately gone to study abroad. For example, Aaron Copland had studied composition in France with Nadia Boulanger, who had taught many other American composers.

However, 1939 was a time filled with constant rumors of war. Furthermore, Germany, the home of many fine musicians and music traditions, where Lenny might have gone to study, was not the place for a young Jewish man. Anti-Semitic laws in Germany had closed Jewish shops and forced Jews out of their jobs in all fields. Far-sighted Jews who could arrange to do so were emigrating away from a country ruled by Nazi laws and hatred. So instead of going abroad, Lenny decided to spend the summer after his college graduation in New York City.

He shared an apartment with his friend Adolph Green and set about to find work. Although he had letters of recommendation, he was not a member of the musicians' union and it was impossible to join until he had been a resident of the city for six months. Lenny managed with an allowance of twenty-five dollars a week from his father. At the end of the summer, he returned to his parents' home, uncertain about what to do next.

It was Dimitri Mitropoulos who at this time suggested that Lenny study conducting. As a result of encouragement from Mitropoulos, Lenny decided to audition for Fritz Reiner, who was the director of the Pittsburgh Symphony Orchestra and who taught conducting at the Curtis Institute of Music in Philadelphia. Other potential students of Reiner's had already auditioned the previous spring. Leonard Bernstein's application was six months late, but Mitropoulos asked his friend Reiner to make an exception and hear Lenny. Reiner was impressed, as Mitropoulos had known he would be. As a result, Lenny received a scholarship to study with Reiner for two years. Sam Bernstein realized that he would have to wait even longer for his son to join him in business. Lenny was busy with a double major at Curtis, conducting and piano.

To a person who knows little or nothing about music, a conductor's job seems simple. They don't play an instrument. Instead, they stand on a raised platform, called a *podium*, in front of the assembled group of musicians: string, woodwind, brass, and percussion players. Conductors wave their arms about while the musicians perform. It looks easy, and it seems more like fun than work!

But, of course, there is much more to conducting than that. The conductor must know what sound each instrument is capable of producing and consider what the composer had in mind while writing the music. The conductor needs to hear each part of the music in his or her head and to know what the whole composition should sound like when it is all put together. The conductor must be able to hear whether every note is played correctly. In addition, the conductor interprets the music, sets the pace for the musicians, and takes the praise or the blame for the quality of each performance of the orchestra. It is hard work, and it is the conductor, not the instrument players, who is seen dripping with sweat at the end of a performance.

Many years later, when Lenny was teaching conducting himself, he described his work: "You have to *play* the orchestra, like you play an organ or an instrument."

In the spring of 1940, Lenny was completing his first year at Curtis. He learned that the conductor of the Boston Symphony Orchestra, Serge Koussevitzky, was starting a summer music school in Tanglewood, Massachusetts. Koussevitzky himself would teach conducting to a few students. Years before, as a teenager, Lenny had attended a concert that Koussevitzky had conducted. As the audience burst into wild applause, he had sat quietly, clapping softly. "Didn't you like it?" his companion at the concert asked him. Lenny had answered, "I'm so jealous."

Now he had a chance to study with the great conductor he admired so much. With recommendations from Aaron Copland and Fritz Reiner, as well as a few other musicians, Lenny applied and was accepted as one of three conducting students at the Berkshire Music Center in Tanglewood. Before long, he and Koussevitzky were more than just student and teacher. A close and lasting friendship was formed that had far-reaching influence on the future of Leonard Bernstein.

Koussevitzky, who had no children of his own, soon looked on the talented, energetic, and handsome young man as a son. He called him "Lenyushka," which was a Russian term of endearment. Like Sam Bernstein, Serge Koussevitzky was a Russian Jew. However, while still in Russia, Koussevitzky had converted to Christianity to further his musical career. He did not suggest that Lenny do the same, but he did advise Lenny to change his name to Leonard S. Burns. He felt it would be better for the young would-be conductor not to flaunt his Jewishness with his name.

Although he listened and allowed himself to be influenced by Koussevitzky in other ways, "Lenyushka" would not deny his Jewish heritage. He felt no need to disguise his background by changing his name. "I'll do it as Bernstein or not at all!" was Lenny's response. Nevertheless, throughout his career, Leonard Bernstein was very insistent that his name be pronounced Bern-STYNE, which is the Germanic way of saying the name, instead of Bern-STEEN, which is the more common Yid-dish pronunciation.

At Tanglewood, Lenny got his first opportunity to conduct a large orchestra. Both of Lenny's conducting teachers, Fritz Reiner and Serge Koussevitzky, used a baton when they led an orchestra. A baton is a thin wooden stick that most conductors wave to indicate the rhythm and tempo of the music and to cue in the performers.

Lenny did not use a baton. Instead he copied Dimitri Mitropoulos, who used only his hands when he con-ducted. Lenny, who had begun his study of music at the piano, said he felt that conducting with his hands was related to the movement of his fingers at the piano.

The next summer, following his graduation from Curtis in 1941, Lenny returned to Tanglewood. By now, Europe was at war and America's involvement was closer than ever. Like other young men of his genera-

Instead of a baton, he used only his hands when conducting.

tion, Lenny had to report to the local draft board. However, the asthma that had disturbed his childhood now made him unsuitable for the U.S. Army. So Lenny was free to continue making music while the rest of the world prepared for war.

For the next two years, Lenny continued to struggle to earn a living as a musician. Although all his teachers and friends in the music world agreed that Lenny Bernstein was a talented musician, it was very hard for him to support himself. For a while, he opened a studio in Boston and attempted to give piano lessons. However, there were not many students and Lenny spent hours writing his own music.

From time to time, he met with Koussevitzky, who continued to encourage his former student. During the summer of 1942, the effects of the war were felt at Tanglewood. The Boston Symphony did not take part in the summer program, but Koussevitzky came nevertheless to lead a student orchestra and named Lenny his assistant.

In the fall of 1942, Lenny returned to New York once again, hoping for better luck. When he ran into a friend in the city, he complained to him that "I am a Harvard graduate, a Curtis graduate, a Tanglewood graduate, and Koussevitzky's assistant, and I still can't find a bloody little job in New York." Amazed, his friend used his influence to get Lenny work making piano arrangements for a music publishing company. For this he received twenty-five dollars a week. Furthermore, the company agreed to publish a clarinet sonata that Bernstein had written and paid him an extra twenty-five dollars a week as an advance on royalties. So although it wasn't much, Lenny was now beginning to eke out a living as a musician in New York City.

In addition, he made money playing for ballet classes and giving lessons. He performed at several concerts. In February 1943, there was a concert devoted to new music at the New York City concert auditorium, Town Hall. Leonard played Aaron Copland's "Piano Sonata." When Lenny had first met Copland, he had played one of the composer's pieces for him. Copland had been delighted and said that he wished he could play his own music as well as Bernstein could. At Town Hall, the audience responded with great applause. Sam Bernstein, who was also in the audience, was overheard to say, "All this applause is very nice, but where is the money?"

August 25, 1943, was Leonard Bernstein's twenty-fifth birthday. It became a very special day in his life. Because of gas rationing in the country, the Tanglewood festival had been canceled for that summer. However, during August, Koussevitzky was giving a series of lectures in Lenox, Massachusetts, and he asked Lenny to come and help him by playing musical illustrations on the piano.

Koussevitzky's wife told Lenny that Artur Rodzinski, the newly appointed conductor of the New York Philharmonic, lived in nearby Stockbridge. She said that Rodzinski wanted Lenny to come and visit with him.

Lenny took the bus to Stockbridge and spent the August night at the Rodzinski home. The next morning, Rodzinski explained why he had invited Lenny to come and visit. Although he had never actually seen Lenny conduct an orchestra, upon the strong recommendation

"All this applause is very nice, but where is the money?"

of Koussevitzky, Rodzinski offered Lenny the position of assistant conductor of the New York Philharmonic. It was Lenny's birthday and he had just received the best present he could possibly ask for. He had a real job at last!

3

Conductor Lenny Bernstein

On paper, Lenny's job as assistant conductor of the New York Philharmonic seemed great. He was working with a famous conductor and a famous orchestra. He had a title and a steady income. His name was printed on the program. However, the truth was, it was highly unlikely that he would ever have the chance to actually conduct the orchestra.

Most of the season's concerts would be conducted by Artur Rodzinski. It was common practice, however, for the major symphony orchestras to invite guest conductors to lead many concerts. Such a visitor might bring a different style or interpretation to a well-known piece of music and offer variety to the musical program. It also gave the musical director some time in which to schedule other concerts for himself in other cities or countries.

Lenny, as assistant conductor, was expected to attend all the rehearsals at Carnegie Hall in New York City. He was there to help Rodzinski and also the visiting conductors. He studied the musical scores and ran errands, even bringing coffee and sandwiches to the conductor during rehearsal. Occasionally, he might take over and conduct during a rehearsal, but he was not expected to do anything more. He was certainly not expected to actually conduct a concert.

On Saturday, November 13, 1943, however, just a few months after he had begun his new job, Lenny was contacted by the Philharmonic's associate manager. He told Lenny that Bruno Walter, who was scheduled to be the guest conductor the following day, was sick with the flu. It was just possible that he would be too ill to take part in the performance. If that happened and if Artur Rodzinski wasn't able to drive through the snow from his Stockbridge, Massachusetts, home to New York City to conduct in Walter's place, then the responsibility would fall to Leonard Bernstein.

It had been about fifteen years since a conductor had been too sick to conduct a Philharmonic concert. So there were two big ifs separating Leonard from taking over the conductor's job. Even without this news, Saturday was an exciting day for Lenny. A composition of his was to be performed that evening at Town Hall.

At the conclusion of the Town Hall concert on Saturday night, Lenny spent many hours partying and celebrating with friends. It was not until the early hours of Sunday morning that he got to bed.

He had not been asleep for long before he was awakened by a phone call. All those ifs had come to pass. He was going to conduct the concert at three that afternoon.

Over the years, accounts have differed about whether Lenny did or did not have time to go over the music for Sunday's concert. Could he have just walked into Carnegie Hall and conducted the New York Philharmonic with no preparation at all? It seems unlikely that he was not shrewd enough to find time to review the scores of Sunday's concert with the intensity of a potential conductor.

When the hour of the concert came, Bruno Zirato, the Philharmonic's associate manager, walked onto the stage at Carnegie Hall. He announced to the audience that Bruno Walter was ill and unable to conduct. He told the audience in front of him they were going "to witness the debut of a full-fledged conductor who was born, educated, and trained in this country." In disappointment, a few people got out of their seats and left the hall. The rest remained in their seats and waited. They were not the only ones who were going to hear the concert. The Sunday afternoon Carnegie Hall concerts were regularly broadcast on the radio. So thousands of people across the country shared the experience of Bernstein's conducting debut.

Lenny's parents and his brother Burton were in the audience. Because they had come to New York City to attend the concert at Town Hall the night before, they were still in the area and able to witness Lenny's second debut in as many days.

"Mr. Bernstein advanced to the podium with the unfeigned eagerness and communicative emotion of his years. He showed immediately . . . his brilliant musi-

The debut of a full-fledged conductor who was born, educated, and trained in this country.

cianship and his capacity both to release and control the players," the *New York Times* reported the following morning.

Burton Bernstein, who was eleven at the time, recalled the concert in his book *Family Matters*. "I don't remember much about the music," he wrote, "except that it sounded all right to me and that Lenny seemed to know what he was doing."

Indeed he must have, for at the conclusion of the concert, " . . . the house roared like one giant animal in a zoo. It was certainly the loudest human sound I had ever heard—thrilling and eerie," Burton wrote.

Lenny came out and bowed again and again to the applauding audience. He even waved to his family sitting in the conductor's box.

Enthusiastic fans, newspaper reporters, and photographers rushed to follow the young conductor offstage. Lenny's amazed parents found themselves being interviewed by the press.

His father, who for years had been ashamed and disappointed with his son's choice of profession, suddenly had something to be very proud of, too. "Just the other day, I said to Lenny, 'If only you could conduct the *Don Quixote*,'" said Sam. "And he said, 'Dad, you'll have to wait ten years for that.'" It is quite probable that Sam Bernstein had never heard of Strauss's *Don Quixote* before his son conducted it that afternoon, but that did not stop his father's imagination from inventing these lines.

The following morning, Monday, November 15, 1943, it was all in the newspapers. Side by side with the World War II news that the U.S. Marines were opening a drive to force the Japanese from the last of the Solomon Islands and that the British Mosquito bombers had attacked Berlin, the front page of the *New York Times* carried the headline

YOUNG AIDE LEADS PHILHARMONIC,
STEPS IN WHEN BRUNO WALTER IS ILL

Music critic Olin Downes wrote, " . . . Mr. Bernstein, on the occasion of the first public concert he ever conducted with a major symphony, showed that he is one of the very few conductors of the rising generation who are indubitably to be reckoned with."

Although the orchestra had been well rehearsed with Mr. Walter, it was clear to Olin Downes that Bernstein "was conducting the orchestra in his own right and not the orchestra conducting him; and though he logically and inevitably conformed in broad outline, he was not following slavishly in the footsteps of his distinguished senior."

Glowing as that review of the concert was, perhaps the *New York Daily News* review was better understood by its readers. The newspaper compared Lenny's substitute performance to a shoestring catch in center field in a baseball game. "Make it and you're a hero, muff it and you're a dope." Lenny had made it!

Incredibly, just a month later, a second guest conductor was too ill to lead the orchestra. So again, Lenny conducted the New York Philharmonic, and again, he got excellent reviews. The music critic Virgil Thomson wrote in the *New York Herald Tribune*, "In previous years guest conductors didn't fall ill. Maybe it is the knowledge that Mr. Bernstein will meet all such emergencies more than capably that enables them nowadays to give in."

In the following months Bernstein also went as a guest conductor to Pittsburgh and Boston. The invitations began to pour in for this young new conductor. Before the year was over, Lenny conducted almost ninety concerts in cities all over the United States.

What caught the attention of the press and music lovers alike was not only that this conductor was a young and unknown man who had unexpectedly and successfully conducted the New York Philharmonic, but also that Lenny was born, educated, and trained in this country. There had been many other promising young conductors in the past. They had gone on to have brilliant careers both in the United States and in Europe, but all of them were Europeans who had been schooled abroad. Their names told the whole story: Arturo Toscanini, Dimitri Mitropoulos, Leopold Stokowski, Hermann Scherchen, Otto Klemperer, Fritz Reiner, Serge Koussevitzky, Artur Rodzinski, and many others. Each was born in Europe, each was a student of European schools and teachers, and each conducted in the tradition of the past.

Leonard Bernstein provided a clear contrast to these venerable leaders in the music world. The Second World War, which had prevented him from traveling and studying abroad, meant that Lenny was not only a native-born American conductor, but one trained here as well.

His style was intense, introspective, and emotional. He twisted and turned his body on the podium. His thick wavy hair fell into his eyes as he moved his head with its strong profile back and forth. His youth and good looks and his energy and passionate movements attracted much attention from the audience. A few years later, when the pop singer Elvis Presley became a sensation because of his gyrations on the stage, some began to refer to Leonard Bernstein as the Elvis Presley of the conducting profession. And like Elvis, Lenny was to develop a huge and loyal following of ardent fans.

The excited and extensive publicity of Lenny's Philharmonic debut and the numerous invitations to be a guest conductor at so many other major orchestras did not please Artur Rodzinski. It created a tension between the two men. Rodzinski was an important conductor, and this was his first year leading the New York Philharmonic. The attention that the music world would ordinarily have given to him was shifted to his young assistant. As a result, Lenny's contract was not renewed for the following year. However, the Philharmonic could not ignore this young man whose career it had launched. Instead, Lenny was invited back as a full-fledged guest conductor.

In addition, during the 1944–1945 season, he served as a guest conductor in Cincinnati, Pittsburgh, St. Louis, Montreal, Minneapolis, Vancouver, and Boston. Sometimes he not only conducted a concert but was the piano soloist as well, leading the orchestra from his seat at the piano. Serge Koussevitzky was proud of the success of his former student. It was his hope that when he retired as the director of the Boston Symphony Orchestra, his protégé, Leonard Bernstein, would replace him.

On his twenty-seventh birthday, Leonard Bernstein was appointed conductor of the City Symphony of the

Sometimes he led the orchestra from his seat at the piano.

New York City Center of Music and Drama. For the ten-week period with two concerts a week that the orchestra performed, Lenny served for no salary at all. He was, however, able to select the music for the series and gain experience working with the same group of musicians over an extended period—an opportunity not ordinarily given to a guest conductor. In his new position, Lenny began including music by twentieth-century composers in his programs. Combining modern music with classical favorites became a hallmark of Bernstein's concerts and influenced other conductors to follow suit.

With the conclusion of World War II, Leonard began to receive invitations to conduct abroad. In the spring of 1946, he made his first trip to Europe and conducted in both Czechoslovakia and England. In addition to leading the London Philharmonic Orchestra in works by American composers, he conducted some music by the nineteenth-century German composer Richard Wagner. It was the first performance in England of any music by Wagner since the British had fought against Nazi Germany during the war. Richard Wagner had died long before the rise of the Nazi government in Germany. But his notorious anti-Jewish attitude and the Nazi admiration for him and his music caused him to be strongly associated with the former German enemy and anti-Semitism. To this day, the music of Richard Wagner causes controversy in Israel.

More important than the fact that he was a Jew, Bernstein's love of music seemed to be the most compelling factor in his life, overriding all other loyalties and emotions. In later years, he visited and conducted concerts in Austria and Germany, although many Jewish musicians, such as Artur Rubinstein and Isaac Stern, made a point of boycotting these countries because of their outrage toward the Nazi atrocities during World War II. Bernstein himself sometimes questioned what he, a Jew, was doing appearing in these countries that had worked to exterminate the Jewish people during the war. Still, despite his ambivalence, Leonard Bernstein returned again and again to these countries. As his reputation as a conductor grew, he was invited more and more frequently to be a guest conductor abroad.

In particular, he led performances in Vienna, where so many of his favorite composers had lived and worked: Mozart, Beethoven, Schubert, and Mahler. It was a great joy to the Jewish-American conductor to be received with such enthusiasm and love in a city steeped in an old music tradition, albeit a city where anti-Semitism had flourished, too.

Still, there was no doubt that Lenny was a Jew. The Jews of Palestine (later Israel) gave him a gala welcome on his first trip there in April 1947. He led the country's symphonic orchestra in Tel Aviv and repeated the program again, as was the custom, in Jerusalem and Haifa. In all three cities, the audience and reviewers alike were enthusiastic about this young Jewish conductor. Lenny himself was so moved to be conducting in the Jewish homeland, the place that he referred to each year at the Passover seder when he said, "Next year in Jerusalem," that he was often moved to tears. Many of the performers in the orchestra were people who had come as refugees to Palestine from Germany and Austria before the start of the Second World War.

Bernstein returned to serve as musical adviser to the Israel Philharmonic during the 1948–1949 season. The newly formed Jewish state came under attack from its Arab neighbors and often the concerts were dangerously near to actual fighting. Lenny, nevertheless, traveled around the country leading the orchestra. One evening he conducted a concert in Beersheba for 5,000 soldiers. Because of the danger, the orchestra was made up only of volunteers, thirty in all. On another occasion, during a concert in Rehovot, there were two air-raid alarms while Lenny was both playing and conducting a Beethoven piano concerto at the same time. He continued playing and his audience sat listening despite the danger. Lenny's courage made him a national hero to the people of Israel. In the years that followed, Lenny returned frequently to conduct in Israel.

A decade later, in September 1957, when a proper auditorium was finally built for the Israel Philharmonic,

Leonard Bernstein was invited to come from the United States and lead the orchestra at the opening concert of the Mann Auditorium in Tel Aviv. The Jewish conductor shared the stage with violinist Isaac Stern and pianist Artur Rubinstein—three Jewish giants of the musical world inaugurating the new concert hall in the Jewish homeland.

As his days became more and more complicated with conducting performances around the world, Lenny realized he needed help organizing his life. Helen Coates, his piano teacher during his teenage years in Boston, came to his rescue. She gave up her teaching and moved to New York City. She began working as a combination secretary-accountant-valet-housekeeper. She booked his schedules, took his phone calls, answered his mail, packed and unpacked his suitcases, and even ran his apartment in the years before he was married.

Three giants of the musical world—Leonard Bernstein, Artur Rubinstein, and Isaac Stern—inaugurated the new concert hall.

Helen Coates was full of devotion and pride in Leonard Bernstein's accomplishments. Every year seemed to bring still more honors to her former student.

Serge Koussevitzky's dream that Lenny would succeed him as conductor with the Boston Symphony Orchestra never came to pass. However, when Dimitri Mitropoulos, who had also been Lenny's friend and mentor, became the musical director of the New York Philharmonic in 1951, he invited Lenny to be a frequent guest conductor. Then, in 1957, at the age of thirty-nine, Leonard Bernstein was appointed co-director of the New York Philharmonic together with Mitropoulos. It was an interesting pairing, for Bernstein was the youngest person ever hired as music director of the Philharmonic and Mitropoulos was nearing the end of his career. Mitropoulos had suffered a heart attack and could not carry the full load of such a job. Indeed, a year later, Mitropoulos resigned his position, and Lenny took over the position on his own. It was an important moment in American music history. He was the first American-born, American-trained music director of an American orchestra. Music lovers waited with excitement for the innovations and freshness they expected of him now that he was working independently.

Ironically, although Bernstein had previously been influenced by Mitropoulos's conducting style and had worked without a baton for the past fifteen years, he changed his image and began using a thin wooden stick when he conducted. He had recently torn a dorsal muscle and conducting with the baton was easier on his back.

One innovation of Bernstein's was the establishment

of a series of "Previews"—concerts at which he spoke informally with the audience about the music to be performed. As in the days when he was conducting the City Symphony, many contemporary American compositions were added to the concert programs. Music by old friends of Bernstein's like Aaron Copland, Ned Rorem, and William Schuman were often performed, as well as music by George Gershwin, Charles Ives, and Roy Harris.

In addition, Bernstein conducted music that he loved by the Romantic German composers. He was personally responsible for reviving the popularity of the music of Gustav Mahler, since he frequently conducted his symphonies. In 1967 he recorded all nine of Mahler's symphonies, which are still regarded as the best interpretations of these works. Bernstein felt a closeness to the late nineteenth-century composer with whom he shared a Jewish heritage, as well as a similar temperament and the dual vocations of composer and conductor. In fact, at one time, Mahler too had conducted the New York Philharmonic.

Bernstein began taking the orchestra on tours to perform around the world, to Latin America, Canada, Europe, and Japan. This brought not only American performers to the rest of the world, but also American music.

Lenny held his position at the New York Philharmonic until he decided, after ten years, to retire from the full-time commitment at the end of the 1969 season. He was then appointed conductor laureate, a lifetime position. It is a position that was awarded him as an honor for all he had done to develop the reputation and importance of the orchestra. It meant that his audience could still look forward to hearing Leonard Bernstein conduct the New York Philharmonic, at least for a few concerts every year. It also meant that his name would continue to be associated with the orchestra regardless of whatever other conducting assignments he undertook.

Traditionally, conductors are called *maestro* by orchestra members. It is an Italian word meaning an important musical composer, teacher, or conductor. Although Leonard Bernstein was indeed a *maestro* by profession, throughout his long conducting career, he was almost always referred to as Lenny by his musicians, music critics, and audiences. Perhaps this is because he started conducting as such a young man. At forty, Bernstein was younger than many of the musicians he was conducting in the New York Philharmonic Orchestra. Furthermore, many of the same musicians were still around from the time, fifteen years earlier, when he had been assistant conductor.

Also, whereas many conductors had a reputation for screaming and intimidating the orchestra by throwing their batons, Lenny maintained discipline without these noisy antics. But somehow, even in later years when his thick dark hair turned to a brilliant white and his face was lined with wrinkles, he was still called Lenny by almost everyone. This familiar nickname did not diminish the feelings of respect or admiration that the musicians felt toward him.

Audiences loved Lenny's energetic conducting style, but there were some critics who complained that he was more a showman than a conductor. When he hugged and kissed his fellow musicians at the conclusion of an

exciting performance, the audience felt he was express-
ing the same pleasure in the music that they had found.
Some critics, however, were embarrassed by what they
felt was an excessive, and perhaps staged, show of emotion. Harold Schonberg, who for many years was the
music critic for the *New York Times*, argued that the
"Preview" concerts were like a music appreciation class,
inappropriate for a major orchestra. He called them
"Young People's Concerts for Old People," and he complained about Bernstein's point of view. The Philharmonic was led by "the Peter Pan of music," he said. He
did not mean this as a compliment!

Furthermore, Bernstein's jumps and leaps on stage,
which entertained audiences, were also felt by some
critics to be unnecessary. Such gymnastics were not the
proper action for a conductor of serious music, they
said. Twice over the years Lenny startled his audiences by actually falling off the podium while he was
conducting.

Yet, despite this criticism, concerts led by Leonard
Bernstein attracted large and enthusiastic audiences.
Throughout his career, he was beloved by his audiences,
who responded to his energetic and passionate approach
to music.

4

An American Composer

At the same time that Leonard Bernstein was making a name for himself as an important conductor, he was also launching a reputation as a composer. Lenny had begun writing original music as a boy. During the summer when he first met Adolph Green at Camp Onota, Lenny had sat down at the piano and played a piece that he told Green was by the twentieth-century Russian composer Shostakovitch. Despite his exceptional memory for music, Green could not recognize the work. He admitted this to Lenny. No wonder! The piece was not Shostakovitch at all. It was a work of early Bernstein. Lenny had a good time fooling everyone else who had heard the music. Green's honest admission that he didn't recognize the music cemented their friendship.

Talented as both a conductor and composer, Leonard

Bernstein spent his entire career juggling these skills within the framework of a 24-hour day and a 365-day year. He could not content himself to be merely a composer or merely a conductor. He needed to be both.

Just as his father, Sam, had expended much energy discouraging Lenny from a career as a musician, Serge Koussevitzky, his musical father figure, discouraged him, too. Koussevitzky berated Lenny for wasting his time composing musicals and writing ballet scores. He felt Lenny should conduct full time.

During the period between his graduation from Curtis and his employment with the New York Philharmonic, Lenny had filled his time composing. A piece that he had begun as a college undergraduate grew into a movement of his first symphony. There is no doubting Lenny's Jewish heritage when you hear this symphony, which he named after the Hebrew prophet Jeremiah. In this work, like Beethoven and Mahler before him, he incorporated the singing of a chorus into the last movement of the musical score. This final movement, "Lamentation," draws on biblical verses for its text. The words are sung in Hebrew. Throughout the work, the knowledgeable listener can recognize the cadences of Hebrew prayers and biblical chants that Lenny had studied as a young boy preparing for his bar mitzvah. When the symphony premiered in this country, the Hebrew was pronounced in the Ashkenazi manner, the way that Sam Bernstein and his friends pronounced the words when they attended services at their synagogue. When the work was performed in Israel, the Hebrew words were sung with the Sephardic pronunciation, which is the way Hebrew is spoken in Israel.

Despite his musical studies at Harvard and Curtis, Lenny never took a course in composition. He did, however, show his music to Aaron Copland and Dimitri Mitropoulos for advice during the early years of his career.

On Saturday evening, November 13, 1943, the eve of his famous conducting debut, Lenny had had another important concert. It was at Town Hall, and it was the first New York performance of a group of five songs he had written for soprano. He called them "kid" songs and entitled the sequence after one of the songs, "I Hate Music."

The soprano voice represents a little girl and the words, also written by Lenny, are quite charming and amusing: "My mother says that babies come in bottles; but last week she said they grew on special baby bushes" begins one of the songs. They were sung by the famous soprano Jennie Tourel. She must have had a lot of fun claiming to the audience, "I hate music! But I like to sing: la dee da da dee." The words are childlike, but the music is sophisticated using jazz influences that would not actually make them easy or appropriate for a young child to attempt to sing.

> Music is a lot of men in a lot of tails, making lots of noise
> like a lot of females;

> Music is a lot of folks in a big dark hall, where they really
> don't want to be at all;

When Lenny had brought the songs to show Koussevitzky the previous summer, the conductor had disliked them. However, the New York music critics had a different opinion, and the song cycle was well received.

It must have been very exciting for the young composer to have his first reviews be good ones.

Shortly after Lenny's conducting triumph, he was approached by ballet dancer/choreographer Jerome Robbins. He had an idea for a new ballet, and he was looking for someone to compose the music. His idea was to show three young sailors on shore leave in the city. The sailors meet and fight over first one and then a second girl. In the end, they all take off after still another girl. As this was the middle of World War II, New York City was full of uniformed sailors on leave. Bernstein could picture the scene vividly. He sat down at the piano and at once began to improvise tunes. Of course, he needed much time to write and rewrite the music. The finished ballet, "Fancy Free," was a wonderful triumph of lively, fresh music. The first performance took place on April 18, 1944, with Lenny conducting.

It was such a hit that it was performed many more times than originally scheduled. During its first season, "Fancy Free" was danced a total of 161 times and it became a part of the standard repertoire for dance companies. In less than six months, the young Jew from Massachusetts had made his mark both as a conductor and as a composer. The name Leonard Bernstein was becoming well known.

As a result of the big success of "Fancy Free," a decision was made to try to expand the ballet into a full-length musical. Lenny's old friend Adolph Green and his talented collaborator Betty Comden agreed to write the book and lyrics. Lenny began to write the music. In the summer of 1944, while he was working on the music for this show, which would become known as *On the*

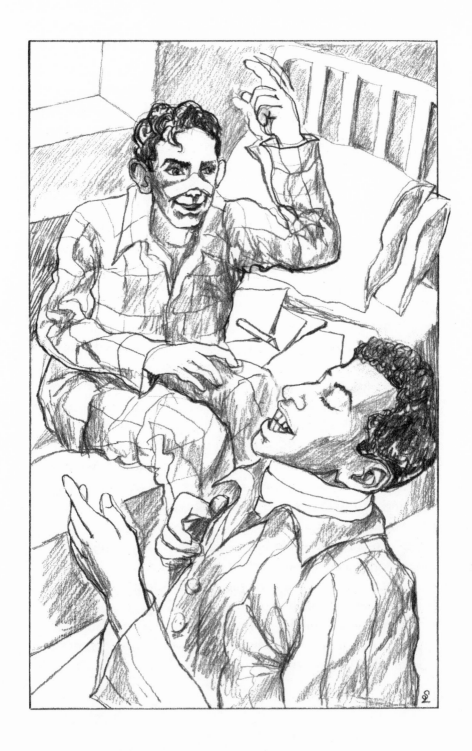

*They shared a room in the hospital and continued
working on the show.*

Town, Lenny needed an operation on his nose for a de- viated septum. Coincidentally, Adolph Green needed to have his tonsils removed. The two young men arranged to have their surgery take place at the same time and in the same hospital. They shared a room in the hospital and continued working on the show while they recov- ered from their separate operations. Leonard Bernstein had too much energy to lie in bed wasting time!

Ballet is a serious art form. Writing music for the bal- let was considered a legitimate way for a serious com- poser to express himself and to make money. Aaron Copland wrote many well-regarded ballet scores. Broad- way musicals, however, do not command the same re- spect in serious music circles.

On The Town was a rousing success and was to be just the first of several popular musicals that Bernstein wrote. Throughout his career, however, there would be criticism of him. What was he? A serious composer or a man who wrote show tunes? A conductor or a composer? Leonard Bernstein seemed to want to be everything.

Lenny composed his second symphony in 1949. It is called "The Age of Anxiety" and was inspired by a long poem of the same name by the twentieth-century En- glish poet W.H. Auden.

The following year, Lenny wrote a one-act opera called *Trouble in Tahiti*, for which he also wrote his own words for the libretto. This was less successful than his *On The Town*. If Lenny worried that he had lost his touch composing music that would be popular, *Wonder- ful Town*, which opened in 1953, reassured him that he was still a successful Broadway composer. For this show

On The Town *was a rousing success. (Source material for this illustration from The Billy Rose Theatre Collection, The New York Public Library for the Performing Arts, the Astor, Lenox and Tilden Foundations; used with permission.)*

he collaborated again with Betty Comden and Adolph Green. It was based on the book *My Sister Eileen*, which had been a best-seller. The musical became a huge hit as well.

In 1956, Lenny's musical *Candide* opened. It was based on the famous eighteenth-century novel by the French writer Voltaire. The show was not very successful at the time. In later years, however, the text for the show was rewritten, and when the musical was restaged, it became much more popular. The overture to the show is often performed at serious concerts.

The work for which Leonard Bernstein seems fated to be best remembered is his musical *West Side Story*, which was first performed in 1957. It is a modern re-telling of Shakespeare's tale of Romeo and Juliet. Two young people fall in love, although their families are enemies. Despite their great love, they are doomed to an unhappy fate. It is a very sad, but very beautiful story. Lenny's music together with the sometimes comic but often moving script by Arthur Laurents and lyrics by Steven Sondheim became a huge box office hit. The show has been restaged all over the world by professional and amateur groups. The music from the show is frequently played on the radio or featured in symphonic concerts. There is hardly an adult in the Western world

West Side Story

who does not recognize the melodies of "Maria," "I Feel Pretty," and the other songs from *West Side Story.*

Leonard Bernstein tried his hand at writing all sorts of music. In 1954, he wrote the background music for the movie *On the Waterfront* and was nominated for an Oscar. The following year, he took this music and shaped it into a symphonic suite.

When John F. Kennedy was to be inaugurated as president of the United States in 1961, Lenny was asked to compose a piece for the occasion. The work for orchestra is entitled "Fanfare." Subsequently, Bernstein was just completing his third symphony, "Kaddish," when he learned of the assassination of President Kennedy. The work for speaker, soprano, mixed chorus, boys' choir, and orchestra was dedicated to the memory of the late president. As *kaddish* is the traditional Jewish prayer for the dead, this seemed a fitting tribute to the slain president from one of America's most popular composers.

It may be said that Aaron Copland's contribution as a composer is more important in American music history than that of Leonard Bernstein. There are other American composers such as Charles Ives and Samuel Barber who have perhaps made more significant contributions in the field, too. Still, Bernstein's music, like his name, is undoubtedly better known by the average American, whether or not he or she is a concertgoer and music lover.

When the Kennedy Center for the Performing Arts was preparing to open in Washington, D.C., the family of the late president commissioned a piece of music from Bernstein. First performed on September 8, 1971, the work, entitled "Mass," is based on religious texts from the Roman Catholic mass. Bernstein described the work as "a theatre piece for singers, players and dancers." Alvin Ailey, the choreographer, planned the dancers' movements. It is perhaps strange to think of a Jewish composer writing a mass. The work, however, was written as a tribute to John F. Kennedy, who was Catholic, and the original concept of using so many art forms within the serious and sober context of the Latin prayers that make up a mass was probably just as startling to Catholics as it was to Jews. Indeed, some critics called the work "blasphemous."

Assessing his friend Leonard Bernstein's music, Aaron Copland wrote in 1960, "At its best it is music of vibrant rhythmic invention, . . . irresistible . . . , often carrying with it a terrific dramatic punch."

It has been argued over and over that if Leonard Bernstein had concentrated on his composition and not split his energies in so many directions, he would have been a greater composer. Certainly, he would have had time to increase his creative output.

In 1957, Leonard Bernstein was the subject of a feature article in *Time* magazine. There he was described as "A Mickey Mantle of music, a brilliant switch hitter, conducting with his right hand and composing with his left." Even the best switch hitters, however, are not equally strong from each side of the plate. To this day, music critics are not in agreement about which was Bernstein's greatest strength. Furthermore, Leonard Bernstein did not limit himself to merely composing and conducting. He also spent time and energy as a teacher, writer, performer, and showman.

5

An American Phenomenon

On September 9, 1951, Leonard Bernstein married Felicia Montealegre Cohn. She was an actress from Chile. Although her father had been Jewish, her mother was Catholic, and Felicia had been raised in the Catholic religion. Before their marriage, Felicia formally converted to Judaism. That was important to Lenny. Their original plan was that they would be married on the lawn of Koussevitzky's home at Tanglewood. Two months before the wedding, however, Koussevitzky died. So the marriage ceremony took place at Mishkan Tefila, the same synagogue where Lenny had chanted the Haftorah on becoming a bar mitzvah twenty years before. Koussevitzky's widow, Olga, gave Leonard clothing that had belonged to her husband to wear at the wedding. Everything Leonard wore, a white suit, pants that were too big, shirt, tie, socks, and even the shoes, had belonged to Serge Koussevitzky.

Felicia and Lenny had three children: Jamie (a daughter), Alexander Serge (named for Serge Alexandrovitch Koussevitzky), and Nina. Felicia was a beautiful woman who had studied piano before she decided to become an actress. Photographs of her with her handsome husband were frequently published in newspapers and magazines. Often Felicia and Leonard Bernstein appeared together on stage when a musical work required a narrator.

The marriage was not without its problems, however, and in October of 1976, after twenty-five years of marriage, the couple separated. Not long afterwards, Felicia was diagnosed as having cancer. She died in 1978. In the years after her death, photographs taken of Leonard Bernstein show him still wearing his wedding ring. Perhaps, like the pair of square gold cuff links that once belonged to Koussevitzky and that Bernstein always wore and always kissed before going on stage to conduct, the ring, too, was a talisman for him, a memory and a link with someone who had been very dear to him.

As a father, Leonard loved to teach and explain things to his children. A simple question from one of the children around the dinner table might lead to a long and involved explanation from their father. When his son was preparing for his bar mitzvah ceremony, Leonard was proud to be able to help him with his Hebrew studies.

Just as he took pleasure in teaching things to his own children, one of Leonard Bernstein's major contribu-

Lenny helped his son prepare for his bar mitzvah.

tions to the world of music was the creation of a series of special concerts for young people, which he began when he was director of the New York Philharmonic. The music was selected for its appeal to children, and the conductor provided a lively commentary explaining what the composer was aiming for and what the musicians were doing.

One of his young listeners later wrote how impressed she was to see the conductor "jumping wildly about, growling like a bear, spitting like an unleashed fire hydrant. And nobody was yelling at him." The audience had great fun at these concerts. With this introduction to music they would not grow up hating it as did the little girl in Bernstein's early song cycle.

Lenny loved this chance to teach. His brother, Burton Bernstein, has said that it was Lenny's favorite occupation. "Descended from rabbis, he was a rabbi at heart, a master teacher." The New York Philharmonic Young People's Concerts were so successful that in time fifty-three such concerts were broadcast on public television. This brought Bernstein's message and face into homes around the country. Television was the perfect medium for this man with the handsome face; a lively, enthusiastic manner; a deep voice that has been compared to a cello; and dramatic flare.

For his appearances on television, Leonard Bernstein received the prestigious Emmy Award nine times. His many lively musical programs on commerical and public television nurtured a new generation of musicians and music lovers in this country.

In addition to his Emmy Awards, he was awarded thirteen Grammy Awards from the recording industry and twenty-one honorary degrees from colleges and universities around the country.

"I think that teaching is perhaps the essence of my function as a conductor," Lenny once said. "I share whatever I know and whatever I feel about the music. I try to make the orchestra feel it, know it, and understand it, too, so that we can do it together."

The musicians on the stage and the children and adults in his audience were not the only ones taught by Leonard Bernstein. In addition, he was on the staff of Brandeis University for several years and a guest lecturer at Harvard University. Furthermore, over the years, he trained many future conductors at the annual summer music festival at Tanglewood. All year long, his conducting students telephoned to speak with him. They asked him what a composer might have been thinking when a particular piece of music was written. He gave them interpretations and moral support, too.

Not content with merely conducting, composing, performing, and teaching, Leonard Bernstein wrote several books about music appreciation. He wrote *The Joy of Music* and *The Infinite Variety of Music*, books that were aimed not at musicians but at the untrained listeners in the music audience.

Somehow, Bernstein found the time to fit each of these activities into his always crammed schedule. Throughout his career, he was able to focus his brain and his energies into three or four separate directions at once. He could study a score, prepare a television script, and work out a new melody all at the same time. He devoted every minute of his life to working, even when he was in taxis, airplanes, railroad stations, and hotel lobbies.

The extrovert Bernstein was always a true showman. In the early days after his Philharmonic debut, he was even offered a Hollywood screen test. He was tested for a part in a film about the Russian composer, Peter Ilyitch Tchaikovsky. According to Bernstein, he was turned down because his ears were too big.

Still, without becoming an actor, he was aware of the value of dramatic gestures, both physically and emotionally. He had several opportunities to conduct concerts of great emotional impact. In 1967, at the conclusion of the Six-Day War in Israel, he was invited to lead the Israel Philharmonic in a musical celebration on Mount Scopus in Jerusalem. It was an exhilarating experience for the Jewish conductor. More recently, on Christmas Day in 1989, he was delighted with the opportunity to conduct Beethoven's Ninth Symphony in East Berlin with musicians from New York, Leningrad, London, Paris, Berlin, Dresden, and Munich. They symbolized the harmony among nations. Their performance celebrated the historic reunification of Germany, which had occurred a few months earlier with the destruction of the Berlin Wall that had divided the city into East and West.

With this in mind, in the final movement known as "The Ode to Joy," the chorus was instructed to change one crucial word: *freude* (joy) was replaced by the word *freiheit* (freedom).

"I feel this is a heaven-sent movement and I am sure we have Beethoven's blessing," the conductor said.

This performance, like so many others led by Leonard Bernstein, was recorded and marketed. In the last years of his career, almost every concert he gave was either broadcast, telecast, or recorded for compact disc.

On November 14, 1988, to mark the forty-fifth anniversary of his conducting debut, he led the New York Philharmonic in an all-Bernstein concert. He did not live to celebrate the fiftieth anniversary.

Although no one knew it at the time, Leonard Bernstein conducted his last concert on August 19, 1990. The orchestra played a work by the contemporary composer Benjamin Britten and Beethoven's Seventh Symphony. Quite fittingly, the concert was at Tanglewood, where Lenny had been a student under Koussevitzky and later a conductor and teacher for more than fifty years. There were other concerts, including a music festival in Japan, listed on Bernstein's calendar waiting for him to lead them, but failing health made him cancel these dates.

Throughout his life, Bernstein was a heavy cigarette smoker. Photographs of him speaking with friends, sitting at the piano composing, or embracing his family almost always show him holding a cigarette in one of his hands. Once his admirers held up a sign for him to read. It said, "We love you—stop smoking." He didn't. He seemed to walk through a cloud of smoke with a cigarette in his hand at every class, interview, or party. Only when he was conducting on the podium were the cigarette and the smoke missing.

His chain-smoking caused him to develop emphysema. It made breathing difficult and brought on uncontrollable coughing attacks. So he suffered during his last years from the same symptoms he had had as an asthmatic child. The emphysema caused progressive lung failure and led to a heart attack, which caused his death on October 14, 1990. He was seventy-two years old.

In addition to canceled concerts and scheduled recording sessions that were never to take place, Leonard Bernstein left many compositions and projects unfinished. One goal he never accomplished was to write an opera about the Holocaust.

Throughout his adult life, Leonard Bernstein's interest in the world involved him in fund-raising for many political and social causes. He gave money generously. Even now after his death, Lenny still provides funds for others. Money from his estate is being used to establish the Leonard Bernstein Center for Education Through the Arts in Nashville, Tennessee. The center's ultimate goal is to train schoolteachers from all over the world in arts education. It is hoped that this will lead to making arts an essential part of every school curriculum.

Early in his career, Bernstein was asked by an interviewer which of his different musical interests he planned to pursue. The answer from Bernstein was that he "wanted to do the thing which seemed the most fun at the time." This response brought criticism. Critics did not seem to think that fun should be the goal of a serious person.

But Leonard Bernstein always took great pleasure in his multifaceted career. Full of enthusiasm, energy, and ideas, it was indeed *fun* for him to leap from one area of music to another.

Perhaps as has been argued, if Leonard Bernstein had concentrated in just one area of music, he would have been a greater composer or a greater conductor. However, Bernstein said of himself that "I don't want to spend my life, as Toscanini [a famous conductor] did, studying and restudying the same fifty pieces of music. It would bore me to death. I want to conduct. I want to

Lenny led four lives in one.

play the piano. I want to write for Hollywood. I want to write symphonic music. I want to keep on trying to be, in the full sense of that wonderful word, a musician. I also want to teach. I want to write books and poetry." So he did, and he had fun doing all these things, too.

After his death, many of his friends and colleagues were quoted in newspapers and magazine articles. Composer Ned Rorem wrote: "Was he too young to die? What is too young? Lenny led four lives in one, so he was not 72 but 288." Composer William Schuman said, "His conducting revealed a maestro so at one with the music that he seemed to have composed it himself. The point of departure was always the creative act, which was present in all his endeavors."

"Lenny is immortal after all," said his brother Burton at the funeral service. "The memories of him will be here, along with the recordings and the revivals and the writings, for generations upon generations." This is true. There are records and compact discs and cassettes of the music he led and the music he composed; thousands of feet of videotape mirroring his face and recording his voice as he lectured. His books are awaiting a new generation of readers. Perhaps, most important, there is a new generation of young conductors, musicians, and music lovers who were inspired by the passionate love of music that Leonard Bernstein spent his life sharing with others.

Important Dates

1918   August 25: Birth of Leonard Bernstein.

1928   The Bernstein family acquires a piano and Lenny begins taking lessons.

1935   Leonard Bernstein begins his undergraduate studies at Harvard University.

1939   Bernstein graduates from college and enrolls as a conducting student of Fritz Reiner at the Curtis Institute of Music.

1939   September 3: France and Great Britain declare war on Germany. World War II begins.

1940   Bernstein spends the summer as a conducting student of Serge Koussevitzky at Tanglewood.

1942   Leonard composes his first symphony, "Jeremiah."

1943   Bernstein is named assistant conductor of the New York Philharmonic under Artur Rodzinski.

1943   November 13: Bernstein makes his debut as a composer with *I Hate Music*.

1943   November 14: Bernstein makes debut as conductor of the New York Philharmonic when Bruno Walter becomes ill.

1944   April 18: The first performance of the ballet "Fancy Free," composed by Bernstein.

1945   August 14: The end of World War II.

1945   Bernstein is appointed conductor of the City Symphony of the New York City Center of Music and Drama.

1946   Bernstein's first trip to Europe as a conductor.

1947   April: Bernstein makes his first trip to Palestine (Israel) and conducts the symphony orchestra there.

1949   Bernstein composes his second symphony, "Age of Anxiety."

1951   September 9: The marriage of Leonard to Felicia Montealegre Cohn.

1953   Bernstein's musical *Wonderful Town* opens.

1956   Bernstein's comic opera *Candide* opens.

1957   Bernstein's musical *West Side Story* opens.

1957   Bernstein conducts the inaugural concert at Mann Auditorium in Tel Aviv.

1957   Bernstein is appointed co-director of New York Philharmonic with Dimitri Metropoulos.

1958   Bernstein becomes the musical director of New York Philharmonic.

1963   Bernstein completes his third symphony, "Kaddish."

1969   Bernstein retires from the New York Philharmonic and is named conductor laureate of the orchestra.

1971   Bernstein composes "Mass" for the opening of the Kennedy Center in Washington, D.C.

1989   December 25: Bernstein conducts in East Berlin to celebrate the destruction of the Berlin Wall.

1990   August 19: Bernstein conducts his last concert.

1990   October 14: Bernstein dies of a heart attack.

AUTHOR'S NOTE

I cannot remember a time when I did not know the name Leonard Bernstein. He was already a grand presence in the musical world when I was growing up. Those were the early days of television, and Bernstein sometimes discussed music on a wonderful new program called "Omnibus." Although we did not yet own a television set, my family made a point of visiting friends and relatives on Sunday afternoons so we could watch this show. As a result, one of the first phonograph records that I ever bought for myself was Bernstein's second symphony, "Age of Anxiety." I became familiar with it when it was used as haunting background music for a dramatization of the life of Abraham Lincoln on that same television program.

While I was still in high school, I attended a concert that Bernstein conducted at Carnegie Hall, and I was thrilled when a friend managed to get Lenny's autograph on my program. To celebrate my college graduation, my parents gave me tickets to one of the most popular shows on Broadway that season, Bernstein's *West Side Story*.

When I was writing this book, I was amazed to see how much had already been written about Leonard Bernstein. Since his famous conducting debut in 1943, he has been the subject of countless newspaper and magazine articles and many, many books as well. There are hundreds of published photographs of him, too, showing him in every pose and every form of dress, from conducting in a tuxedo to walking along a beach in a pair of swimming trunks.

When you read as much about someone like Lenny Bernstein and see so many pictures of him and have heard him speak on many, many television programs, you begin to feel as if you have really known him. Yet the closest I ever got to Leonard Bernstein was to glimpse him sitting in an office in Lincoln Center just before a concert some years ago. Still, I feel as if I have spent much time in his presence. I feel as if I sat in a room inhaling the smoke from his cigarette and watching and listening as he spoke to me. I saw him gesturing and speaking enthusiastically about his passion for music. That passion, together with his recordings and compositions, is what Leonard Bernstein has left as his legacy to all of us.

BIBLIOGRAPHY

Bernstein, Burton. *Family Matters: Sam, Jennie and the Kids.* New York: Summit Books, 1982.

Bernstein, Leonard. *Findings.* New York: Simon & Schuster, 1982.

Briggs, John. *Leonard Bernstein: The Man, His Work, and His World.* Cleveland: World Publishing Company, 1961.

Copland, Aaron. *Copland on Music.* New York: Doubleday & Company, 1960.

Gradenwitz, Peter. *Leonard Bernstein: The Infinite Variety of a Musician.* Leamington Spa [UK]: Berg Publishers, 1987.

Gruen, John. *The Private World of Leonard Bernstein.* Text by John Gruen. Photographs by Ken Heyman. New York: Viking Press, 1968.

Peyser, Joan. *Bernstein: A Biography.* New York: Beech Tree Books (New York: William Morrow & Company), 1987.

Schonberg, Harold. *Facing the Music.* New York: Summit Books, 1981.

Other sources included articles printed in various newspapers and magazines, including the *New York Times*, *Newsday*, *Time* magazine, *Classical*, and *Rolling Stone*.

INDEX

"Age of Anxiety, The," 45
Ailey, Alvin, 49
Anti-Semitism, 15–16, 33

Barber, Samuel, 48
Beethoven, Ludwig van, 33, 34, 55, 56
Bernstein, Alexander Serge, 51
Bernstein, Burton, 6, 9, 26, 28, 53, 59
Bernstein, Jamie, 51
Bernstein, Jennie, 5, 7, 10, 14
Bernstein, Leonard
  academic ability of, 9
  as asthma sufferer, 5–6, 20, 56
  audience reaction to, 38, 39
  as author, 54

birth of, 5
called "Lenny," 5, 38
changes his name from "Louis," 5
children's concerts by, 53
children of, 51
as composer, 40–49
  of "The Age of Anxiety," 45
  of *Candide*, 46
  of "Fancy Free," 43
  of "Fanfare," 48
  of "I Hate Music," 42
  of "Kaddish," 48
  of "Lamentation," 41
  of "Mass," 49
  of *On the Town*, 43, 45
  of *Trouble in Tahiti*, 45
  of *West Side Story*, 47–48
  of *Wonderful Town*, 45–46

Bernstein, Leonard (*continued*)
as conductor
of City Symphony,
31–32
education for, 16–17
guest appearances by,
30, 31
of New York Philhar-
monic, 23, 24, 25,
26–29, 31, 36–37
style of, 19, 30–31, 36,
38
travels abroad, 32–35,
55
critics of, 38–39, 49, 57
death of, 56
develops emphysema, 56
early interest in music
of, 6
education of
at Boston Latin School,
9
at Curtis Institute of
Music, 16, 17
at Harvard University,
14–15
at New England Conser-
vatory of Music, 9
at Tanglewood, 18, 19
first symphony of, 41
forms own musical group,
11
fund-raising by, 57
in Israel, 34–35, 55
as a Jew, 18, 33, 34, 41
job searching of, 16, 20
last concert of, 56
likened to Elvis Presley, 31
marries Felicia Montea-
legre Cohn, 50

modern music in concerts
of, 32, 37
newspaper reviews of, 26,
28, 29–30, 42–43
at New York Philharmonic
assistant conductor, 23,
24, 25
co-director, 36
conducting debut,
26–29
conductor laureate,
37–38
guest conductor, 31, 36
music director, 36–37
organizes own musical
productions, 12
piano lessons for, 8, 9, 10,
11–12
piano lessons taught by,
10, 20
at piano practice, 3, 5, 8, 10
"Preview" concerts of,
36–37, 39
pronunciation of name of,
18–19
receives Emmy Awards, 53
receives first piano, 8
receives Grammy Awards,
53–54
receives honorary degrees,
54
recordings of concerts by,
55
rejected by army, 20
shyness of, 6
as smoker, 56
studies conducting, 16–17
at synagogue, 6–7
as teacher, 51, 53, 54
unfinished work of, 57

versatility of, 57, 59
works as musician, 20–21
Bernstein, Nina, 51
Bernstein, Sam
  admiration of, for Leonard, 12
  at conducting debut of Leonard, 28
  discourages Leonard from musical interest, 3, 5, 8, 10–11, 41
  religious background of, 6
  at Town Hall concert, 21
  values education, 14
  wants Leonard to join his business, 5, 12–13, 14, 15, 16
Bernstein, Shirley, 6, 9, 10,12

Candide, 46
Coates, Helen, 11–12, 35–36
Cohn, Felicia Montealegre, 50, 51
Comden, Betty, 43, 46
Copland, Aaron
  assesses Leonard's music, 49
  ballet scores of, 45
  as composer, 48
  gives Leonard advice, 42
  Leonard performs music of, 21, 37
  meets Leonard, 14, 21
  recommends Leonard for Tanglewood, 18
  suggests composing to Leonard, 15

"Fancy Free," 43
"Fanfare," 48

Gebhard, Heinrich, 11
Gilbert and Sullivan, 12, 15
Green, Adolph
  Leonard performs for, 40
  meets Leonard, 15, 40
  shares apartment with Leonard, 16
  writes *On the Town* with Leonard, 43, 45
  writes *Wonderful Town* with Leonard, 46

Harris, Roy, 37

"I Hate Music," 42
Infinite Variety of Music, The (Bernstein), 54
Ives, Charles, 37, 48

Joy of Music, The (Bernstein), 54

"Kaddish," 48
Karp, Frieda, 8
Kennedy, John F., 48, 49
Klemperer, Otto, 30
Klezmers, 5, 11
Koussevitzky, Olga, 50
Koussevitzky, Serge
  assisted by Leonard, 21
  conducting style of, 19
  death of, 50
  discourages Leonard from composing, 41
  as European conductor, 30
  Leonard's son named for, 51
  recommends Leonard to Rodzinski, 21, 23

Koussevitzky, Serge (*cont'd*)
  suggests Leonard change
    his name, 18
  at Tanglewood, 17, 20, 56
  treats Leonard as a son, 18
  wants Leonard for Boston
    Symphony Orchestra,
    31, 36

"Lamentation," 41
Laurents, Arthur, 47
Leonard Bernstein Center
  for Education Through
  the Arts, 57

Mahler, Gustav, 33, 37
"Mass," 49
Mishkan Tefila, 6, 50
Mitropoulos, Dimitri
  conducting style of, 19, 36
  as European conductor, 30
  gives Leonard advice, 42
  meets Leonard, 15
  at New York Philhar-
    monic, 36
  suggests conducting to
    Leonard, 15, 16

New York Philharmonic, 23,
  24, 25, 26–29, 31, 36–37

On the Town, 43, 45

Rachmaninoff, Sergei, 11
Reiner, Fritz, 16, 18, 19, 30

Robbins, Jerome, 43
Rodzinski, Artur
  as European conductor, 30
  makes Leonard assistant
    conductor of New York
    Philharmonic, 23
  meets Leonard, 21
  at New York Philhar-
    monic, 24, 25
  and tension with Leonard,
    31
Rorem, Ned, 37, 59
Rubinstein, Artur, 33, 35
Ryack, Eddie, 9

Scherchen, Hermann, 30
Schuman, William, 37, 59
Sondheim, Steven, 47
Stern, Isaac, 33, 35
Stokowski, Leopold, 30

Tanglewood, 17–18, 19, 20,
  21, 56
Toscanini, Arturo, 30, 57
Trouble in Tahiti, 45

Wagner, Richard, 33
Walter, Bruno, 25, 26, 29
West Side Story, 47–48
Wonderful Town, 45–46
World War II, 15, 19–20, 28,
  30, 32, 33, 34

Zirato, Bruno, 26